Sarah,

Opal

Almost Perfect Angels

almost Perfect Angels

31 SPIRITUAL LESSONS
MY GRANDCHILDREN TAUGHT ME

Rose Otis

Pacific Press® Publishing Association
Nampa, Idaho
Oshawa, Ontario, Canada
www.pacificpress.com

Edited by Tim Lale

Cover and inside text design
by Linda Griffith

Back cover photo © Photography by Dale

ISBN: 0-8163-1925-1

02 03 04 05 06 • 5 4 3 2 1

Dedicated to

Grandpa Bud,
my loving husband,
and to Heidi,
my daughter,
and to Heather,
my granddaughter,
and to Leesa,
my daughter-in-love.

If it weren't for each of you,
I wouldn't have had a reason
for writing this book!

Lovingly,
Your wife, mother, grandmother,
and mother-in-love,

Rose

FOREWORD

When life seems too difficult to handle, I often reflect on something that has brought joy to my life. Sometimes it's a funny expression or comment that one of my children has made that makes me smile again. In this book, my mother has compiled thirty-one of these special moments that will give the reader a unique view into the joys of grandparenting.

She doesn't only remember the good times. She also reflects on circumstances that have at times seemed too overwhelming to tackle. But with God's help, amazing things have happened.

In today's society there are too many broken families and families separated by long distances, far from a parent, grandparent, or treasured loved one. For these reasons I encourage you to demonstrate your love and build security in creative ways such as email messages, postcards, or a quick phone call to wish your grandchild a good day. These inexpensive forms of communication can allow children to experience a rich relationship, even from a distance, with loved ones from another generation who have so much to give.

This book includes stories drawn from memories of questions asked and experiences shared. It's a look inside the pride you feel when your grandchildren are successful and the pain you share when they struggle. You may recall the quiet times, the sad times, the fun times you've spent creating that special bond. And in reflecting, you catch a glimpse of the love and pride God must feel as He sees us desiring to have a closer relationship with Him. Yes, you can work all your life in a powerful job and not enjoy the same fulfillment you can experience from being a loving, supportive grandparent.

Let me remind you of what God says in Psalm 127:3: "Behold, children are a heritage from the Lord" (NKJV). I hope you will hug your child, or grandchild, a little tighter, kiss them more often, and always hold on to those special memories you've made together!

Happy reading,

Heidi Otis Bresee, *Mother of Ryan, Heather, and Eric*

CONTENTS

INTRODUCTION

Each time I learned that I was going to be a grandmother my heart literally skipped a beat (well, at least, it felt like it)! I discovered that our first-born was on the way when I was speaking at a women's meeting in Texas. During the lunch break, I went to a phone at the back of the lodge and dialed my daughter's home number. Soon she answered and, standing at the pay phone I got some of the biggest news of my life. I was going to be a grandmother! The subsequent three were equally welcomed. Notably the little "post script" who came along after an eight-year gap.

In my state of euphoria, I recall telling another grandmother that I didn't think a person could have too many grandchildren. The woman looked at me in disbelief. "Try twenty-seven at Christmastime," she said, "and you might change your tune!" She may have had a point there—but then I'd already been assured that this would never be a concern of mine!

What would he/she call me, I mused as I walked back to join the meeting—Gran Gran, MeMaw, Granny? I remembered reading a long list of names that grandchildren called their grandmothers that included "Big Bertha"! Please, spare me little one, I thought. Well, as I write this book I know what my "grandmother" names are—so far.

They're Grandma Rose, Grammy, and Gramzy, and I gladly answer to them all!

Rose Otis

1
"IS IT OVER?"

God's timing is perfect!

Some of my favorite weekends include a visit from our grandchildren. Their grandpa and I have many special memories of their visits from infancy to the teen years.

When the eldest, Ryan, was a three-year-old he loved to spend the night at our house, especially since he had a room he called his own. But he went through a period when he became convinced that there were wolves upstairs. According to him, he had actually heard them growl, and he even claimed to have seen their big eyes! No amount of convincing erased the fear of a night visit from the wolves.

So we came up with the idea of using the mattress from a crib in an adjoining room to make Ryan a bed on the floor beside Grandpa and Grandma's bed. Need I say that this was a popular decision?

When my husband and I had made up the "floor bed," the three of us knelt to pray that the wolves would be kept at bay throughout the night. We showered Ryan with hugs and kisses, and I had just tucked in his covers when I felt a little hand reach out. "Grammy," he said, "let's hold hands." So we did.

It seemed that only a short time had passed

when the next thing I knew there was some movement from the "floor bed." I opened my eyes. Through streams of morning light creeping in around the window shades, I saw Ryan watching me. He was kneeling on his bed, and his big blue eyes just cleared the top of our mattress. He asked me a simple question. "Is it over?" Now, in his mind that meant "Is the dull night over?" That period of time when playfulness ceases and Grandpa lies still in his bed instead of playing hide-and-seek. To a three-year-old, nighttime is a dreadful waste of time, and when it's over—that's incredibly good news! As for me, I can't remember a night that felt too long. But I couldn't help smiling at my grandson. "Yes, Ryan," I said, "it's over!"

Time is relative, isn't it? It all depends on one's situation. For instance, our degree of tiredness or our age may determine whether or not we're ready for the night to be over. This same concept applies to our spiritual life as well. Sometimes I feel like crying, "Lord, is it over?" Because I'm tired of the pain I see, and the separation, and the painful situations people get caught in in this world. But then there are other times when I want to plead just as urgently, "Lord, wait just a little longer!" That's when I sense my own need to come closer to Him or when someone I love isn't walking with the Lord.

There's only one Person we can trust to know when it's time for the "night" to be over, and that's our heavenly Father. Just when the timing seems right for me, it may be wrong for you. He and He alone will know when there's been enough night. But for now, He's given us today to get ready for the glorious morning of His soon coming—when there will be no more night. Praise Him for His loving-kindness!

2
FIRST AFTER YOU!

It's important to put others first.

As parents and grandparents we spend considerable time teaching our children good manners, to share with one another and others, and to learn the skills of getting along and not always having to have one's own way. No small task to be sure. In fact, the only persons who think otherwise are those who have yet to raise a child.

When Ryan was about six years old and his sister, Heather, was four, he thought himself too old to play with a four-year-old—especially a four-year-old girl. On the other hand, she adored him. In fact, she was willing to play his games or with his toys just to have his company.

His mother and I had commented on this a number of times. How clever he was, Heather thought, when he built his tall Lego towers. She would sit on the floor and just watch. One day when the two had been playing together especially well I overheard a little exchange I've never forgotten. In fact, I used it in a sermon I preached at the 1995 General Conference Session.

In the midst of what seemed idyllic, Ryan decided he'd had enough and announced that he was going to go do something different. Heather was on her feet immediately, and as she hurried to catch up with her brother, I heard her say, "Ryan, I'll play whatever you want to play, and I'll be first after you if you'll play with me."

"First after you!" I've smiled as I've thought of those sweet words. In this world you're either first or you're second, third, fourth, or something on down the line. But little Heather, with her blond curls bouncing, was willing to be second—or "first after Ryan" in order to have his companionship.

How sweet would this world be if we were all willing to be "first after one another." Or if everyday we looked for ways to put a smile on the faces of our family members, coworkers, and friends. What if we went out of our way to be inclusive? Of course I can't be sure, but I wouldn't be surprised if the phrase, "I'll be first after you" would be a very familiar term in the new earth!

3
DID JESUS CHUCKLE TOO?

Jesus wants all of you!

The family had gathered in the living room of our home to view a video that featured the story of the good Samaritan. Our three grandchildren sat patiently through the long introduction until finally the story began. The room was quiet except for the narrator's voice until Jesus came onto the scene. Our three-year-old grandson jumped up and began pointing at Jesus on the television screen.

"That's Jesus!" he shouted with obvious delight. "He's the one who lives in my stomach. Right, Mommy?" he said, pointing to his own small tummy.

"Yes, sweetheart, that's a picture of Jesus. But Jesus lives in your heart, not in your stomach. Remember?"

"Oh, yes. He lives in my heart, and I live in His heart too," he said with all the conviction a three-year-old could muster.

The rest of us tried to stifle our giggles. His older brother and sister looked around the room at the adults who were struggling to keep straight faces, but Eric was right. Jesus lives in us and tells us that we are on His mind and in His heart too. I like to think that Jesus had a good chuckle over Eric's wrong choice of organs, and then rejoiced that one to whom "the kingdom of heaven belongs" wanted Jesus to live in him.

Come into my heart today, Lord Jesus, and into my mind, and yes—even into my stomach. For You have created my body to be a temple of the living God, and the God of my life must live in all of me.

4
A Gift for the Baby King

LESSON FOUR:

Jesus loves to receive gifts too!

I walked up and down the aisles of the department store pushing my four-year-old grandson, Ryan, and his two-year-old sister, Heather, in a shopping cart. The store was crowded with holiday shoppers, and my daughter, Heidi, was trying to make a few last-minute selections before Christmas. Now if you've ever tried to keep two small children corralled in a shopping cart for any length of time, you know that thirty minutes can seem like twenty-four hours! For when you've managed to capture one child's attention, you discover the other precariously straddling the cart in an attempt to examine something you can ill afford to take home in one piece, let alone a hundred.

That day I discovered that one of the safest aisles in the store was the one displaying brass items. While my grandchildren sat like little angels surveying the passing merchandise, I tried to keep the cart moving fast enough to prevent them from grabbing anything and yet slow enough to make the trip down this particular aisle last as long as possible.

Ryan wanted to examine a decorative brass French horn. I saw no harm in his request, and after a few imaginary blasts on the horn he put it back on the shelf. Beside it, though, was a lovely octagonal-shaped brass box with a delicately pierced, cone-shaped lid. "Oh, Grammy," Ryan called out with a sound of awe in his voice. "Look, it's just like the box at the manger, isn't it?" he said, pointing at the beautiful brass container.

I had to admit that he was right. The ornamental brass box did look like something a wise man might have brought to Bethlehem. "You're right, Ryan," I said, picking up the box to examine the detail. "It does remind me of the gifts the wise men brought Baby Jesus."

With a sense of wonder Ryan traced his small fingers over the design, seeming to want to prolong the moment. When he was through examining it, we carefully placed our newfound treasure back on the shelf and continued down the aisle. I leaned over the cart and gave my little grandson a big hug. For it was he who had reminded me that the true spirit of Christmas is not long lists of "to-do's," busy shopping malls, and plastic credit cards, but a celebration of the arrival of the greatest Gift of all—Jesus, our Lord and Savior.

5
THE BIG SNEEZE

LESSON FIVE:

Things are often not as bad as they seem!

Clay is our youngest grandchild. He came along on April 14, 2001, as a bonus grandchild. Our son was forty years old when Clay was born, and he and his lovely wife, Leesa, are thrilled to be parents. I remember my son saying soon after Clay's birth, "Mom, I'm a father. It doesn't get any better than this!" Looking at the joy spread across his face, I nodded and readily agreed. Parenting is one of God's greatest gifts to humankind, and He understands our pride and joy because He too has a Son.

When we have recalled Clay's arrival the family has had some good laughs at how we behaved over having a new baby in the family once again. When Clay was first born we all vied for the "opportunity" to change his diapers. However, that has changed in recent months.

Clay is a curious little boy with big blue eyes that you never tire of looking into. On a recent visit to Grandma and Grandpa's house he was lying on a blanket on the floor while his mom and I were fixing lunch. Grandpa was on the couch beside him, watching Clay with one eye and CNN with the other. It was then that Clay was first introduced to the "big sneeze." Without warning Grandpa let out one of his earth-shattering sneezes, momentarily taking Clay's breath away and then sending him into a terrified crying spell. Once we had consoled Clay, we adults had a good laugh, all agreeing that Clay had better get used to Grandpa's "big sneezes" because he is bound to experience more in the future!

Reflecting on Grandpa's "big sneeze" and little Clay's reaction, I thought to myself—there are times when life seems calm with no major threats on the horizon, when without warning something happens that puts us in a worry mode and may even bring us to tears.

Grandpa's sneeze reminds me of a lot of things in life. While they may appear to be scary in the short run, often our fears are unwarranted. The devil likes to send us on a wild goose chase to get us off track. However, keeping our eyes focused on Jesus will bring peace. We can claim this biblical promise that is as true today as when it was written thousands of years ago. "And the peace of God, which transcends all understanding, will guard your hearts and your minds in Christ Jesus" (Philippians 4:7, NIV).

6
MARKED!

Jesus loves you just the way you are.

When our grandson Eric was about three years old he was at the neighborhood swimming pool when a little girl, not much older than he was, stopped to stare at the small birthmark on his upper forehead. And then, being brutally honest, she said, "Hey, kid, you have a duck on your forehead!"

Eric was stunned. When he regained his composure he ran to where his mother was seated to tell her of the cruelty he had just endured. He started out calmly but ended up in tears. The thought of going through life with a duck on his forehead was more than he could bear.

God gives mothers wisdom just when they need help. And He put words in Eric's mother's mouth. "That tiny brown spot is a kiss from Jesus," she said confidently. "He gave it to you so that every time you look in the mirror it will remind you of how much He loves you! You are very special to Jesus." Eric listened thoughtfully then dried his tears and went back to his play.

Recently, five years later, Eric was visiting us. He was playing with other children who were also visiting, when I heard one of them say, "Eric, you have something on your forehead."

"No," he said matter-of-factly. "It's just where Jesus kissed me!" The little girl looked at him with astonishment. Her expression said, "Wow! Jesus kissed you on your forehead. You must be somebody special!"

There are persons I admire a great deal who are physically challenged in some way. I draw strength from them as I sense, in a small way, what it has required of them to be the person they've become. Jesus is marked too! Throughout eternity He will bear the nail prints in His hands as reminders of His sacrifice for our redemption. " 'This man was handed over to you by God's set purpose and foreknowledge; and you, with the help of wicked men, put him to death by nailing him to the cross. But God raised him from the dead, freeing him from the agony of death, because it was impossible for death to keep its hold on him' " (Acts 2:23, 24, NIV).

I don't know where or how Jesus "kissed you" and made you special. But if you know Him as your Creator, Redeemer, and soon-coming Savior you should feel very special indeed! If you don't, make it your top priority. Because understanding why He will wear the nail scars in His hands, forever "marked" for our sakes, will transform your life!

7

LONGING FOR REASSURANCE

Everyone needs to know that they're not alone.

I agree with what Carl Sandburg had to say about babies, "A baby is God's opinion that the world should go on." How could it be expressed any better than that!

Clay, our youngest, is still a baby, but how quickly he is growing. If I don't see him for a week I can see changes. This past weekend he had discovered how to reach out with both hands and grasp something I held. I even noticed how he would reach up and scratch his head! Wow! Those little four-month-old baby fingers were getting pretty clever. I never tired of holding a toy up to him and seeing his eyes focus and then watching his hands respond by reaching out to take the toy and guide it straight to his mouth. Babies haven't changed much, I thought, as I smiled at this little boy of ours.

And that wasn't all he'd learned that week. He'd found out that he had a voice, and he enjoyed using it. It usually happened when he was in his crib or left to play on a blanket on the living-room floor that we'd hear him babbling. We noticed that with time, he'd begin to increase the volume. And then suddenly, without warning, he'd let out a single high-pitched screech and then wait, with his big blue eyes wide open to see if he was going to get any action. And he would! We were all so amused that he had discovered a way to call us that one or more of us would show up at his crib-side. It didn't take him long to figure that out either. Every time he repeated this little ritual that weekend, he charmed us with his obvious intelligence.

When the weekend came to a close and we'd tucked him in his car seat for the two-hour journey home, we had another good chuckle over how he brought the household to attention with one single baby-size shriek. Did he need some evidence that he was not alone? Did he just want some reassurance that we loved him and would come to him whenever he needed us; or was he just having fun trying out his newly discovered vocal cords?

I'm not sure, but this experience reminded me of how I respond to my heavenly Father. When I'm feeling alone I say a little prayer asking Him to come close to me and take away my anxiety. There are other times I raise the volume and the intensity of my pleading, when a situation becomes more urgent. And then there have been situations in my life when, like Clay, I cried out to my heavenly Father for reassurance that He knows where I am and will not leave me! And wonder of wonders, I have discovered that there will never be that one rare moment when He'll leave me. " 'Never will I leave you; never will I forsake you' " (Hebrews 13:5b, NIV).

Someday I'll tell Clay about his first tries at verbalizing and how he entertained us so. I'll tell him how we couldn't resist responding by picking him up and showering him with love. And I'll also tell him about a heavenly Father who knows each of His children by the sound of their voice—including his.

8
LOVE RETURNED

Love is a two-way street.

It had been a day to remember. When less than twenty-four hours old, our newest grandson, Eric, had come home. For the first few hours we all took turns examining his tiny toes, button nose, and funny-looking tummy button. At the time his older brother Ryan was four years old and sister Heather was a two-year-old. They were Eric's most devoted fans!

Finally at bedtime my daughter, Heidi, offered her two older children a reward for getting ready for bed without delays. The reward—one last chance to hold their new brother! It was a prize they couldn't resist. Soon they both reappeared bathed and pajama-clad. With obvious delight they took turns cradling the newest member of the family. What fun!

When it was Ryan's turn, his mother suggested that because he was the big brother he could hold the baby on his shoulder—the way she liked to hold him. So with one hand supporting tiny Eric's head and the other around his waist, Ryan rocked the baby.

All of a sudden the baby began to awaken. Arching his neck and drawing up his legs, he began to squirm in Ryan's arms. When Ryan felt his brother moving against his own small chest he called out excitedly, "Look, Mom, he's loving me back!"

Many times since, I've thought about this simple exchange between two brothers and Ryan's delight over Eric's unconscious movements—accepted as his own love returned. How wonderful to be "loved back" by a loved one or a friend. How we search for this response in even the simplest acts.

In a beautiful book entitled *The Desire of Ages,* I discovered a moving description of how our Savior longs to be "loved back."

> Our redeemer thirsts for recognition. He hungers for the sympathy and love of those whom He has purchased with His own blood. He longs with inexpressible desire that they should come to Him and have life. As the mother watches for the smile of recognition from her little child, which tells of the dawning of intelligence, so does Christ watch for the expression of grateful love, which shows that spiritual life is begun in the soul (p. 191).

9
FIRST IMPRESSIONS

A father stands in the place of
God in his children's eyes.

I was blessed to be able to spend fifteen years as a stay-at-home mom when our two children were growing up. It was a choice that required some minute budgeting and determination on the part of both my husband and I. But as I look back on life, I believe it was one of our better decisions.

When I did enter the workplace I became involved in various roles of ministry. I remember working at our church world headquarters at the time of a special "Week of Prayer" that was conducted for the employees. Dr. Miroslav Kis was the guest speaker, and he spoke to my heart.

One morning he began by telling us that our image of God was framed early in life. He said that if father spanks then God spanks. If father reasons then God is reasonable. If father is absent then God is likely to be absent when you need Him. If father loves then God is loving. If he is fair then God must be fair. However, if he is always busy, or even abusive, then God may not be available and worse yet may even be feared.

And then, having said this, he threw out a chal-

31

lenge to those of us in the audience. "When you go home," he said, "take a piece of paper and ask your child to draw a picture of God!" He went on to say that if father were tall God would be tall. If father's bald, God won't have hair on His head, and so on.

Well, our children were grown, but I couldn't wait to try this experiment with one of our grandchildren. So, when Heather came to spend Sabbath with me I sprung it on her. Taking a piece of $8\frac{1}{2}$" x 11" paper, I placed it in front of her and gave her a pencil. "Heather, draw Grandma a picture of God!" I suggested. She looked at me as if I had challenged her to roller skate on Mars. "Go ahead, your picture doesn't need to be perfect. Just draw what you think God might look like." I said. "Grandma's curious."

Hesitating momentarily, she stared at the blank piece of paper lying in front of her. And then haltingly she lifted the paper that had been lying horizontally on the table in front of her and turned it vertically. And I got goose bumps! Heather's father, Daniel, is six feet four inches tall. She went on to give God long arms and legs and big feet and curly hair. Dr. Kis had been right! Six-year-old Heather had drawn a sketch of her earthly father.

But here's the good news. If the picture of your father is not perfect, it's because we live in a sinful world. It's a world in which the effects of sin have left their mark for generations. But this isn't the end of the story. Rejoice with me! God has promised that He is eager to re-parent us and to give us a clearer understanding of who He is. So, if our first impressions were not all they should have been, remember that they don't constitute the final chapter—unless we allow them to.

10
I'M TIRED OF BEING A PUMPKIN!

LESSON TEN:
This world is not our home.

It was Halloween, and the children in my daughter's neighborhood were looking forward to wearing costumes and visiting each other's homes to collect a sweet of some kind. Because of traveling a great deal in my work, I had missed three Halloweens. So I was looking forward to spending the evening with our three grandchildren. I finished work and hurried to their home, where I had to take a second look to recognize my grandchildren.

Six-year-old Ryan was dressed like G.I. Joe, complete with face paint. Heather, age four, had borrowed her mother's emergency nurse attire, and with a stethoscope bouncing along as she ran, she informed me that she was a "docto." Her R's were not always detectable.

And then there was Eric, two-and-a-half, who stole the show in his pumpkin suit—a round, puffy, orange costume with holes for arms and legs. To top it off, he wore a hat with green petals and a stem. He was ready to go in search of the treats with a plastic pumpkin in hand—except for one thing. He wanted transportation! He made a convincing appeal to Grandma that he needed to be carried in order to keep pace with the older kids.

I felt as though I was the one who needed to be carried, but I succumbed to his pleading and swooped up my precious pumpkin. So he did some walking, and I did some carrying in our hopeless attempt to keep up with his two older siblings. After about two blocks of this routine he came off the porch of one house, sized up the small stash in his plastic pumpkin, and announced, "Grammy, I'm tired of being a pumpkin!"

"So soon?" I asked.

"Yes, I want to go home." So home we went.

I've thought about this simple little exchange between a toddler and his sanguine grandmother who enjoys making analogies out of experiences just like this one. How often we get "dressed up" for the day, full of anticipation, hoping the new day will bring good things such as quiet time with God, gifts of friendship, time with loved ones, the opportunity to learn something new, a new chance at life! But, in spite of all the possible outcomes of a new day, there are times when, like Eric, we are tempted to say, "Lord, I'm tired of being a pumpkin. I want to go home!" For the costumes we wear on earth are only borrowed. But the King of kings is fashioning beautiful robes of righteousness in my size and yours. And since He "knit us in our mother's womb" in a variety of colors and sizes, each robe will be "one-of-a-kind." An original in the finest sense of the word!

And I hope that the finishing touches are being put on mine, because just like Eric, "I'm tired of being a pumpkin!"

11
A GRANDPA QUESTION

LESSON ELEVEN:

Be ready to give an answer.

You could see the shadows lengthening as Grandpa and Ryan made their way down through the hills and dales of northern Virginia to Grandpa and Grandma's house. Ryan had made this trip even before he could remember.

This time he had taken up his position behind his grandpa, seated on a little jump seat that he called his own. While the pick-up's passenger seat offered more comfort, the jump seat offered a private corner of the world. Like a fort on wheels!

It was during one such journey, in the midst of silence and creeping shadows on the forest floor outside his window, that Ryan asked the question we still talk about. "Grandpa, do trees move?"

After a thoughtful moment Grandpa asked, "What you do mean by 'move,' Ryan?"

"Well, do they move around in the forest after dark?" Ryan added. A smile, and perhaps a tear, came across Grandpa's face. His little grandson, who had been quiet for some time, was exploring some rather deep thoughts for a pre-schooler. And Grandpa had the privilege of telling Ryan that trees have deep roots through which they get their nourishment and these roots hold them in the same place throughout the life of the tree.

Grandparents and grandchildren have a special relationship that our heavenly Father wants to nurture. An old African proverb says, "We need to give our children two things—roots and wings." But before these roots can go down there needs to be some "soil preparation." Having grown up on a farm, and being an avid gardener in his adult years, Ryan's grandpa understands the necessity of preparing the soil before planting. Cultivating children and grandchildren can involve playing a game of Monopoly, putting a worm on a fishing hook, teaching a child to water ski, and making every effort to show up for the big events in their lives. Now that's fun cultivating!

The author of the Psalms speaks of children as arrows. "Children are a gift from the Lord; they bring real blessings and joy into the home. The sons and daughters a man [woman] has during his [her] adult years will be security for him [her] in old age, just as many arrows in a quiver are security to a warrior. Happy is the man [woman] who has many children [grandchildren and great-grandchildren] because they will stand by him [her] when he [she] needs help" (Psalm 127: 3-5, TCW).

Al Hartley, author of *It Takes a Family*, said, "Noah was the first grandparent to build a lifeboat out of the family tree. God called it an ark! God is still using arks—patri-arks and matri-arks"*—or grandfathers and grandmothers. Perhaps more today

---

*From *It Takes a Family*, by Al Hartley, published by Barbour Publishing Inc., Uhrichsville, Ohio. Used by permission.

than at any other time our children and grandchildren need the security that an extended family can provide. They need security in the form of answers to their questions and a continuous cultivating process. This healthy course contributes to a sense of belonging and healthy self-worth that must be nurtured and passed on by the next generation of matri-arks and patri-arks.

While writing to Timothy, the apostle Paul spoke of Timothy's rich inheritance. "I have been reminded of your sincere faith, which first lived in your grandmother Lois and in your mother Eunice and, I am persuaded, now lives in you also" (2 Timothy 1:5, NIV).

12
WELCOME HOME, CHILD

LESSON TWELVE:

*Heaven becomes more real when you picture
yourself opening the door to your heavenly mansion
and finding a loved one there.*

My husband and I were busy building a small get-away place on a lovely wooded lot overlooking a lake in northern Virginia. It was to be a place where our family could gather to find quietness together amid the smell of the woods, the changing seasons, and the glassy lake inviting an early-morning ski.

I looked for opportunities to drive down to the lake to see the progress the builders were making. On one such trip I took my granddaughter, Heather, who was about four years old at the time. What joy she found in discovering that the house now had a roof and window openings cut into the walls. To her the whole process seemed magical. Only a couple of weeks earlier we had gone down and found only a hole in the ground where the basement would be someday. Ever since she could remember, Heather had come to this spot to swim and picnic. She had even taken her first try at water skiing and loved it! And now, as if it had appeared at the wave of a magic wand, a house stood on the property. A house with walls and a roof and so many places for a child's inquiring mind to investigate.

I began by taking her on a little tour of the roughed-in house to familiarize her with the layout. "Heather, we can celebrate Christmas here this year," I said. "Come, help me decide where we should put the Christmas tree!"

Without a moment's hesitation she walked toward the front door, pointing to the floor. "Right here will be perfect!" she declared, pointing to the small foyer just inside the door. "Then everyone who comes will be able to see it!"

Trying to keep a straight face, I could only imagine guests struggling to get past the tree and into the house if I were to take her suggestion to heart.

And then a delightful game began. "Grandma, I have a great idea!" she shouted from outside. "I'll come to the door and knock, and you pretend that you are surprised I have come for Christmas, OK?"

"Sure," I responded, realizing that there were several possible entries into the house, including the basement, and being sure that she wouldn't miss one of them.

Knock, knock. "Oh, Bud!" I would say excitedly, pretending that her grandpa was along and in on the game. "Someone is at the door." Hurriedly I criss-crossed the rooms, each time answering the appropriate door with a shriek of delight. "Grandpa!" I would call back into the unfinished house. "It's our Heather. She's come for Christmas! Come in, my darling, and give me a hug. Oh, it's so wonderful to see you!"

Then she would cross the room to where she had positioned the imaginary tree and begin to exclaim over its beauty. "Oh, Grammy, look at the golden angels! Aren't they beautiful? And look at all the presents!" she exclaimed, stretching her arms as wide as they'd reach.

Again and again I answered the various doors, each time stopping to swoop her up into my arms and welcome her home. Dress rehearsals for the real thing. It was her first visit to Grandma and Grandpa's new house, and her dancing eyes and playful heart had lit a fire in an unfinished house that would linger as long as memory lasts. A loving child of ours had come home. What unspeakable joy she brought to our hearts!

My heavenly Father is preparing a real mansion for me in the new earth. And now in my mind's eye, just like Heather, I run to that mansion door and knock and picture Him answering the door and finding me there.

"It's me!" I say with Heather's exuberance and picture the twinkle in His eye when He lifts His voice and calls, "Look, it's Rose! She's come. She's come home!"

Yes, Heather has taught me the overwhelming joy at the sight of finding a loved one at your door—any door! The anticipated response of being welcomed with open arms. Oh, come, Lord Jesus. Come!

13
TAKING A LEAP!

Jesus is our real lifeline!

Our family and friends were enjoying an annual get-together at our home on Virginia's Lake Anna when one after another decided to enjoy a twilight swim. Some went in the water appropriately attired, while others, the younger set, began to toss one another off the dock and into the warm water clad in casual clothes. Our two oldest grandchildren were immediately caught up in the innocent fun and immediately leaped off the dock to join the others already in the water.

The youngest, Eric, watched with great interest. Walking to the edge of the dock and pointing at the dark water, he asked me a simple question: "Gramzy, what's in there?" I assured him there were some fish in the lake but that it was the same water he had spent much of the afternoon splashing in. It just looked different because he couldn't see into the water without sunshine.

After watching the others running and jumping into the water, letting out hoots of delight when they surfaced, he could stand it no longer. "Gramzy, I want to go in too, but I want you to go with me," he said.

"Go ahead," I urged him. "You'll like it! Your brother and sister are in there."

He was not easily convinced. I watched as he walked to the edge of the dock and peered down at those he envied and then stepped back to survey the whole situation. Finally, when he could stand it no longer his eyes fell on a ski rope neatly wound in a circle, lying unattached on the dock. He walked over and, taking the end of the rope, he wrapped it around his waist twice with great care. Then, walking to the edge of the dock, he jumped into the water. Soon he forgot all about the rope around his waist, having conquered his fear through his trust in a powerless rope.

How often have I reached out to grasp false security when I couldn't see the future clearly? I knew Eric was safe because he wore a life jacket and because I was watching him closely. I also knew that the rope he clung to offered only superficial security.

I wonder how often our heavenly Father smiles as He sees His children reach out to grasp false security, knowing all along that their safety is sure under His watchful eye. What peace this offers. An ever-vigilant heavenly Father watching over His children—including you and me.

14
CHEATERS NEVER REALLY WIN

LESSON FOURTEEN:

Playing by the rules is the only way to go.

My husband had taken Ryan, who was ten at the time, to play a round of miniature golf. We were living in Texas, and even a temperature above 100 degrees didn't temper Ryan's enthusiasm to play at a fairly new miniature golf course that sported life-size giraffes and zebras. Surrounding the miniature golf course were other activities to tempt children and drain parents' and grandparents' wallets—racecars, boats, and ice cream shops.

Soon Ryan and his grandpa were into their golf game. On one particular hole players were to hit the ball through a tunnel and then take a path that went up a small man-made mountain to see how close they had come to putting the ball in the hole—the object of the game! Ryan had never played on this course, and so while Grandpa added up the score, Ryan hit his ball through the tunnel and then ran up the miniature mountain path to see the results. Just when Grandpa began to wonder where he had gone Ryan came hurrying back down the path to announce "Grandpa, I hit a hole-in-one!"

Something about the look in Ryan's eyes told

Grandpa that the hole-in-one had had a little help from Ryan.

"Ryan," Grandpa said. "You didn't really shoot a hole-in-one, did you?" Ryan looked down, embarrassed over having been caught in his attempt to achieve a low score.

"No," he said. "I didn't, Grandpa."

"When you ran over the 'mountain,' did you put your ball in the hole?"

"Yes, Grandpa, I did," Ryan responded with his lower lip trembling.

"All right, Ryan, let's play this hole over again the right way!" Grandpa admonished. Ryan placed the ball on the rubber mat and swung the club, sending the ball sailing through the tunnel to its unknown destination. Together he and Grandpa scampered up the "mountain path" to see how they had faired. Much to his surprise, Ryan could see his red ball in the cup!

Indeed, he had hit a hole-in-one! Turning to his grandpa with a look of awe on his face, Ryan said, "You're right, Grandpa! You don't have to cheat to win!"

15

THE SOUND OF HIS VOICE

LESSON FIFTEEN:

Jesus will calm your anxiety when you turn to Him in troublesome times.

What could be more fun than a rope swing that could take you on a ride out over the lake, where you'd drop into warm water, exhilarated by the experience and eager to get in line for another turn? The bigger you were, the farther out your weight would carry you, and the smaller you were the shorter the ride.

One Sunday morning Grandpa took the grand-children to a favorite spot not far from our house. He went early so the line would be short and the younger children could have a turn. Ryan and Heather took turns climbing the bank and grasping the rope that propelled them out across the water. When they let go there was a squeal and a big splash. Grandpa sat nearby enjoying the fun.

But one of Heather's turns went sour. When her feet left the ladder and she began to swing out over the water, she noticed her younger brother who was wading in the shallow water. Although he posed no danger, from her viewpoint she thought she was going to hurt him if she didn't let go prematurely, and so that's what she did—sending her diving face first into the shallow water.

Immediately, the adults feared the worst. Blood

flowed from her nose and mouth. Her Aunt Leesa was the first to get to her and lifted her gently from the water into the boat. Heather was sobbing quietly until her grandpa took her in his arms and began to console her. "Heather, listen to Grandpa. It's very important that you lie still here while I take you back home to your mommy. Grandpa and Aunt Leesa will be right here beside you."

"OK," she said, stifling her tears. They laid her on a soft towel in the center of the boat and headed home.

Nearing the dock, Grandpa called for our daughter to come quickly. Heidi is a pediatric nurse practitioner. She sees a lot of severely injured children in the PICU of Shady Grove Adventist Hospital in Rockville, Maryland.

When I saw Heather's bloody face, I felt like fainting. But her mother stayed calm. "Come here, sweetheart. Let's have a look at this pretty face. Oh my, it looks like you may have cracked a bone in your little nose. Let's have a look at this lip," Heidi said, opening Heather's mouth to examine her lip, tongue, and teeth.

Grandma got ice. We were all praying for this little girl who loved adventure and swam like a fish, but now lay quietly while her mother checked her pupils and other vital signs. A call to the doctor and another one to the pharmacy, and everyone moved into action to assist someone we dearly love.

When we were sure that Heather's injuries were not serious, Grandpa said, "Heather, Grandpa was so proud of you. I know that you were hurt and afraid, but you listened and did exactly what I told you to do. I'm very proud of you!" He stooped to kiss her forehead.

"I stopped crying and laid still because I knew you would take me to my mommy, Grandpa. I just knew you would help me."

Why? Because all through Heather's young life, Grandpa has been one of her best supporters. His confident voice and strong arms gave her strength in a time of fear.

The other day when we rode by the rope swing there was a long line of kids waiting their turn. "Heather, look," I said. "Look at all those people lined up just waiting to break their noses!" She could laugh then, but she's lost all interest in rope swings.

When we're in trouble we want assurance that we're not alone. When we call out to our heavenly Father we can be certain that He hears us. And while we can't see Him physically we can be sure that He is watching over us. At times we feel His presence even through silence. Just as Heather has learned to trust her earthly grandfather, our heavenly Father wants us to place our confidence in Him. And this confidence comes by building a relationship with Him day by day. I once heard someone say that God takes emergency calls when He recognizes the voice! As His children we can be sure He knows our voices, and knowing this brings peace that this old world cannot offer!

16
READ A STORY ABOUT ME!

Angels are recording our life stories.

It was bedtime, and Eric was less than eager to call it a day until I suggested that if he'd take his bath and get into his pajamas quickly, I'd read him a story about a boy named Eric!

He was very curious. He didn't know that there was such a thing as a story about Eric, but he was eager to hear it if there were such a thing. Washing himself from head to toe, he then dived face down under the water for a quick rinse and barely stopped to run the bath towel over himself. He called out from his bedroom, "Are you sure there's a story about Eric? It's not this Eric, is it?" His eyes sparkled at the possibility of such.

"There sure is, and you're about to hear it!" My answer delighted him!

When I came into his bedroom, I found him propped up on a couple of pillows and waiting, all ears! I had decided to read him an experience that involved him from one of a series of women's devotionals that I had contributed to. As I read, he hung on every word and regretted that the story wasn't longer. I promised that I would read another the following evening and, having said our prayers, I kissed him goodnight.

49

Each night we repeated this ritual. And every night he waited eagerly for another story that included him. Finally, on the last night that he was to spend at our home, I searched the devotional books to find one last story that mentioned him, but to no avail. The closest I could come was a story about his brother and sister. The disappointment was obvious. "I'm not in the story, Gramzy?" he inquired.

"No, Eric, you're not. And the reason you're not is because you weren't born when this story was written!" Well, it was difficult to argue the point any longer. So I read the experience involving Ryan and Heather, but his level of enthusiasm had taken a dip.

Then I remembered one other book in which there might possibly be something I had written that included all three children, and I hurried out of the room to look for it. Sure enough there was, and when I announced that I had discovered one, he was all smiles! I didn't need to remind him to be still and listen. He had snuggled up with his head next to my pillow and was listening intently.

After we'd had prayer and I was saying goodnight to this special little boy that Jesus kissed on the forehead, I thought about the books in heaven that the angels are writing in every day of our lives. And I paused to tell Eric that an angel was writing down the story of his whole life and that someday when Jesus comes to take us to heaven, he'd be able to read the stories that a real angel wrote about him. We discussed how thick the book might be, and whether the angel ever got tired of writing or was ever disappointed in what he had to write down, and even how beautiful his handwriting must be. Eric assured me that he's eager to read the most important story of his life. And I determined that I didn't want to miss out on that story either!

17
TELLING MARKS
ON THE WALL

LESSON SEVENTEEN:

*Don't erase the milestones of childhood for they are
what make the man or woman.*

We had lived in our new retirement home full time
for less than a year, but already I found myself think-
ing about giving the kitchen a fresh coat of paint.
One morning, with sponge in hand I went from wall
to wall removing smudges and small fingerprints
until I came to the wall next to the refrigerator. Here
I put down the sponge and paused to scan the various marks on the wall and the story they told. "My,
how time flies," I said aloud to myself. The tale
began with a small mark that didn't reach my knee.
I knew that it indicated that Clay was twenty-three
inches when he was first measured. The precious
marks stepped all the way up the wall and stopped,
temporarily, at 5' 3"—a mark belonging to Ryan!

Ever so often either my husband or I will back
the children up to this wall, making sure their heels
are flat on the floor, and placing a ruler on top of
their heads we mark the progress of their growth—on
their journey to full stature. And for some of these
small fries, full stature could mean a mark somewhere
around 6' 4"—-their father's height. Wow! Sharpen

the pencil. We've got a ways to go, but as I survey the current progress we're well on our way!

I picked up the sponge and continued to clean. I smiled as I recalled one of my own childhood memories. Quite frequently during our adolescence years, my brother John, who is two years younger than me, would want me to stand back-to-back with him in front of the medicine cabinet mirror. This ritual was followed by a groan of disappointment over what he was convinced was his fate in life. He was sure that he'd never be as tall as I was. Well, he was wrong! He's at least 6' 1".

We place a lot of emphasis on measuring physical growth, when actually this measurement is of little importance in the wider sphere of life. The question that really matters is, are we growing in the spiritual growth category? "And Jesus grew in wisdom and stature, and in favor with God and men" (Luke 2:52, NIV). How well do those little heads that press up against the ruler, wanting every fraction of an inch coming to them, understand God's wise and generous plan for their lives? Now that's a question we need to be asking ourselves every day.

On September 11, 2001, terrorists struck on the soil of "the land of the free and home of the brave." From that moment on, regardless of age or socio-economic status, we've all felt vulnerable. There have been times when my mind has gone to our children and I find myself saying, "What if the terrorists strike again in such a way that we'd be separated from the children?" Well, I've known for a long time that "what if's" are one of the evil one's viruses that, when allowed, will run rampant inside one's faith. For children of the King know that nothing is too hard for God!

" ' "Ah, Lord God! Behold, You have made the heavens and the earth by Your great power and outstretched arm. There is nothing too hard for You" ' " (Jeremiah 32:17, NKJV)! And once again I decide to stick with my Lord—to put the children in His care.

And so when buildings tumble from the sky in front of my eyes on the television, over and over again I will run to the shadow of His wings. "How precious is Your lovingkindness, O God! Therefore the children of men put their trust under the shadow of Your wings" (Psalm 36:7, NKJV). Wow, I want my grandchildren to know where to run without a second thought. To the cool, protective shadow of Your mighty wings, Father!

I don't know why we are surprised when the world around us is going crazy. Jesus Himself told us that it would be this way. Yet, somehow even His children seem to think they are entitled to a trouble-free life. So, when trouble comes knocking we can be devastated.

When the world around us is in chaos and there's nothing we can do to change these circumstances, little acts of love mean all the more. A hug; some quiet time at bedtime to read together and answer questions; an "I love you sooo much, Grandma," from Eric on his way out the door to the school bus; a time to rock our baby and reflect on a world to come that will be free of fear. " 'These things I have spoken to you, that in Me you may have peace. In the world you will have tribulation; but be of good cheer, I have overcome the world' " (John 16:33, NKJV).

I'm not certain of too many things, but there's one thing I am sure of. When Jesus comes to call His children home the only measurement He'll look for is the depth of our love and commitment to Him. So, while the world heaves and groans its last breath, let's use these fleeting moments to stamp impressions of the things our children and grandchildren need to understand and practice in order to be ready to meet Jesus! Let's help them see that God has a far wider plan for their lives—a plan that can't be measured by the human mind. Inspiration says it this way: " 'For I know the plans I have for you', says the Lord. 'They are plans for good and not for evil, to 'give you a future and a hope' " (Jeremiah 29:11, TLB). So, grow, little ones, grow, and may you always measure up to the stature God has planned for you!

18
So Much Fluff

When you are afraid, call upon Him.

Ryan and Eric had come to spend the weekend with Grandpa and Grandma. We always attempt to accelerate our own energy levels in order to keep up with these two lively, growing boys. Ryan was eleven and Eric seven when this episode took place.

We'd had an especially busy day, and when it was bedtime no one had to coax any of us to shower and turn in for the night. I offered the boys the opportunity to stay in the guestroom on the same level as our bedroom, with the condition that they'd settle down and go to sleep. Although they both readily agreed to do so, having been a mother of small children, I decided to check on them before turning in. I knew that putting them both in the same king-size bed was waving temptation's tail in front of them. So I quietly made my way down the hall and stood outside the door that was slightly cracked open and listened to the following conversation.

"I'm scared, Eric!" Ryan said.

"Oh, Ryan, what are you scared of anyway?"

"I'm scared of all the things I can't see out there in the dark," Ryan said, motioning toward the large window beside the bed.

"Oh, I can't understand you, Ryan," said Eric. "I'm four years younger than you, and you are the scaredy-cat."

"Yeah, but you're by the door, and I'm here next to the window," Ryan countered.

"Well, I wish you'd just stop making me scared and go to sleep, Ryan," Eric said, turning his back to his brother. "And did you forget that I have my big St. Bernard right here in bed with us?" questioned Eric.

"Right! And your big dog is full of cotton!" Ryan's voice was sarcastic.

I had to leave immediately and stifle my laughter. How true! Eric had this huge stuffed animal in bed with him, but that animal was powerless to do anything to protect the boys, and Ryan was quick to remind him of the fact.

How comforting to know that we have angels who watch over us and an omnipresent heavenly Father who keeps a watchful eye over His children. No, we don't serve a God that's full of cotton but an all-powerful, almighty God who created us. He knew our names while we were yet in our mother's womb (see Isaiah 49:1, NIV). He cares about little things like two little boys afraid in the dark. How do we know? Because He assures us by telling us that He even knows the number of hairs on our heads (see Matthew 10:30, NIV). Each of our names is engraved in the palm of His hand (see Isaiah 49:16, NKJV). We need not be afraid because we are of inestimable value to Him. How do I know this? Because the Bible tells me so! Jesus died so that we can be where He is and live eternally—without fear. "And this is the testimony: that God has given us eternal life, and this life is in His Son" (1 John 5:11, NKJV).

19
PICTURE PERFECT

My family teases me about all the photographs I take. It's one of my favorite hobbies. After all, in order to qualify as a "super grandma" I have to be able to produce photos at a moment's notice. And I can. Just ask me!

Any grandparent worth their salt can bore the socks off others with a fistful of photos. We can't help ourselves—it seems to come with the title. But have you ever wondered why we're the ones who carry around the pictures of our grandchildren and they couldn't produce one of us if you turned them upside down and emptied their pockets?

However, I learned that there is a reason behind this phenomenon. Al Hartley, a Christian author, shed some light on this subject when he said, "Love flows down. Down from the throne of the universe, down from the cross, down through generations, down to the youngest member of the family." This explanation explains why grandparents are the ones who carry the photographs.

One night while our seven-year-old grand-daughter, our only granddaughter, was spending the night with me I invited her to share our big king-size bed. What a "picture perfect" experience for a grandma. Grandpa was going to be gone overnight, and Heather jumped at the chance to occupy his spot. When it was time to go to bed she got in on his side and scooted over until she was lying right beside me.

"Let's talk," she said. Well, while I hadn't come to bed to talk I could tell she wasn't ready to go to sleep, and there are few people I enjoy talking to more than Heather.

After we chatted a bit in the darkness I asked her, "Heather, do you know what you need to do to be ready to go to heaven when Jesus comes?"

"Tell me," she said. So I began to identify various principles and truths, and as I named each one she responded enthusiastically, "I do that!" And when our little "heavenly conversation" was drawing to a close she sat up in bed and, with obvious joy, said, "I'll get to go, won't I, Grandma?" And then without hesitation she continued, "Grandma, you have to tell Ryan and Eric just what you told me. I mean it! Because they aren't doing all these things, and I want them to go too!"

Heather wanted to make certain that her brothers didn't miss out on the unimaginable plans our heavenly Father has planned for His children. She wanted to spread the good news while there was yet time!

I doubt that we'll have cameras in heaven. There'd be no need. We will have perfect recall. This in itself is something to look forward to, particularly for those of us who qualify for senior-citizen discounts here on earth. However, we're told that when we do get to heaven we'll spend eternity recalling special moments like the one I had with Heather. It was a "picture perfect" opportunity to enrich her spiritual training as Jesus did when He encouraged the little children to come close to Him, when He mingled with our ancestors' grandchildren while living down here on earth.

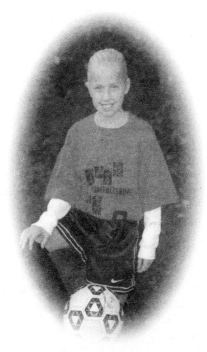

20
CONQUERING YOUR FEARS

Never fail to thank God for helping you to conquer a fear.

I've heard it said that the third child has some challenges that the first two may not face. But I've also read that it's not so easy to be the middle child and that if you're the eldest you must be an example and bear added responsibility. So, since we have absolutely nothing to say about our birth order, we make the best of it!

When Eric was seven years old he was aware that the members of his family were avid water-skiers, and he felt some pressure to learn to ski. His older brother reminded him that he already new how to ski by the time he was seven, and he'd better rustle up some courage and get up on those skis.

So, one day Grandpa asked Eric if he'd like to try to ski. He promised that Uncle Todd would get in the water with him and help him get his skis on and teach him how to begin skiing. Eric thought about the invitation for a few minutes and decided to take the plunge.

After two or three tries he found himself actually "skiing on water." His face showed sheer terror, but he hung on for dear life and survived a big circle back to his Uncle Todd, where he let go of the rope and dropped into the water. Everyone on the dock was clapping and shouting their accolades over his accomplishment. When he surfaced and discovered that he had skied and lived to tell about it, a broad smile came across his face.

That evening as the family gathered for a meal, Eric made a big pronouncement. "I feel a big prayer coming on, and I know just what I'm going to say. Can I say the prayer?" he asked. Obviously, we were all waiting to hear the "big prayer" that Eric wanted to deliver to Jesus in the midst of his family. So taking hands, we listened as he thanked Jesus for the good day, for his family, for the food, and then came what we'd all been waiting to hear—"the big prayer."

"And thank You, Jesus, for helping me to be a skiing boy too!"

Eric is an exceptionally good swimmer, but for some reason the thought of balancing on two wooden boards and flying across the water was frightening to him. But he had conquered his fear—faced it down and survived! And that was the reason behind the "big prayer" he felt coming on!

21

LOOKING FOR
HEAVENLY FIREWORKS

LESSON TWENTY-ONE:

*Prepare now so that your family will be on
hand for the biggest fireworks display of all.*

Our neighbors have come to know that the Otises
celebrate with fireworks. Why? Because one young
man, our eldest grandson Ryan, is especially fond of
them. So, on Memorial Day, the Fourth of July, Labor
Day, and Christmas, and any other reason he can
find to celebrate, the skies over our front yard are lit
with shades of red, green, gold, and white punctuated with loud booms!

I remember last Christmas well. After sharing
gifts and enjoying Christmas dinner together, Ryan
hastened to invite us to observe his fireworks display.
Most of the family stood back on the bank leading
down to the dock, where the fireworks were set off
over the lake. Each barrage of color was followed by
exclamations over their unique beauty as the dying
embers fell from the sky like so many falling stars
into the black lake waters.

Even before he was too young to participate in
lighting the fireworks, his enthusiasm was much the
same. The flash of light when the wick caught fire
and then a moment of silence before the boom! He

almost seemed to hold his breath while waiting to see the colorful pattern of each firework explode. Yes, it's true. Ryan was "bitten" early, and he never fails to make sure that we have fireworks on hand to punctuate these special holidays.

The Bible describes a time when the heavens will be lit to celebrate the coming of Jesus. In Revelation we can read about a "Hallelujah time!" "Then I heard what sounded like a great multitude, like the roar of rushing waters and like loud peals of thunder, shouting: 'Hallelujah! For our Lord God Almighty reigns. Let us rejoice and be glad and give him glory!' " (Revelation 19:6, 7, NIV).

When reading Revelation I get a clear impression that God is inviting His children to the grandest display of fireworks ever assembled! The heavens will be lit by thousands of angels as they accompany Jesus coming to take His children home.

Patri-arks and matri-arks everywhere need to pray for opportunities to teach young inquiring minds what's essential in order to be invited to this wedding feast. Ryan's Grandpa and I want to do our part to make certain that he has a front-row seat for this once-in-a-lifetime extravaganza of light and sound. In fact, it's our desire that each one of our family members—and yours too—will be on that invitation list!

22
PASSING THE BATON

Remember how important it is to pass on the values and skills you've learned to the next generation.

The phone rang. It was 7:30 A.M., and I wondered who was calling so early. It was Heather. "Grandma, I have a quiz today, and I have to identify ten fabrics. Mom said to call you; she thinks you'll know the answers. And you know, Grandma, I want to get 100 percent!"

"OK," I said. "Give me the question and the possible answers, and I'll see what I can do!"

"The first one is brocade," she said. "Do you know what brocade is, Grandma?"

"Read me the descriptions, and I'll tell you which one describes brocade," I said. We went down the list, and my granddaughter was glad that I could help her toward her goal of 100 percent on the quiz.

I smiled as I hung up the phone. In my mind's eye I could see myself seated on a small cane chair in front of my Grandma Jennie's treadle sewing machine. I can still see the name of the manufacturer on the black machine. My first assignment was to make an apron. Grandma made sure that even with this rather simple task I took time to press the seams open and gather the waist evenly. I was rather pleased with the results.

A few months later Grandma asked if I would like to make a dress that I could take to academy with me in the fall. It sounded like a daunting task, but with her help I felt confident that we would be successful. I can still remember her driving me to town in her wine-colored Studebaker to purchase the fabric. We ended up buying some soft pink cotton with a sheen and tiny pin-sized white dots. The choice of a pattern presented an even more difficult decision for me. For the first time, I realized that I would have to put a zipper in the dress. With not a small amount of trepidation I asked the clerk for my size in the pattern we had selected and then watched as she unrolled the soft fabric and cut just the right amount for my next big project.

Fortunately, Grandma Jennie was a patient person. She never scolded me, no matter how many times I had to pick out the zipper in order to get it even. Her calm words of encouragement gave me the desire to continue with the project until I tied off the last thread and proudly held up the finished product. Grandma made me feel that I was the one making the dress and she was just the coach!

I didn't know at the time that in just a few years I would be married with two children. With my husband's encouragement I decided to be a stay-at-home mom. This decision required some fine-tuned budgeting. Consequently, an exciting day for me was a day when I'd find a fabric sale and buy three-quarters of a yard to make my little girl a sun suit. Because Grandma Jennie had taken the time to "pass the baton," Heidi and I had wardrobes that would have been prohibitive if they had been store bought. But as my mother would say, we did it on a shoestring!

And so, yes, I did know what brocade was, and chiffon, and poplin. These were foreign words to Heather, but they were like old friends from the past to me—because someone took the time to teach me a skill I would use throughout my life.

Grandma Jennie sleeps in a little country cemetery in northern Michigan. When Jesus comes, she and I will have so much catching up to do. But I hope I remember to thank her for teaching me to garden, sew, make bread and homemade pies, can tomatoes, and make blackberry jam—things that have enriched my life long after she was gone. "For we are God's workmanship, created in Christ Jesus to do good works, which God prepared in advance for us to do" (Ephesians 2:10, NIV). I like to refer to these good works as mentoring the next generation or "passing the baton."

23

HOME-SCHOOLING AT JESUS' HOUSE

LESSON TWENTY-THREE:

*You can't go wrong
if you follow Jesus' example.*

Summer was coming to a close and school would soon be in session again. How quickly the years come and go! I still remember the smell of new crayons, the feel of a new pair of shoes, the big decision over choosing a new lunch box. What fun! But this year was going to be different for Eric.

He was going to be a second-grader, but first grade had revealed that he was facing a big challenge for a little boy. Eric had a reading disability. So while Ryan and Heather were readying themselves to board the yellow school bus the opening day of school, Eric was adjusting to the fact that he was going to be home-schooled. Mom had quit her job and was devoting much of her time to teaching Eric. She hadn't realized how much he struggled to read until she sat beside him day after day. The first couple of weeks were the most difficult. Eric missed his friends. He wanted to ride the bus too. "I just want to feel normal!" he said one morning. Mom assured him that he was normal and tried her best to hide her tears.

As they began to work on phonics and word

exercises, Eric got in the habit of asking his mom for a hug and a kiss before he would begin his lesson. He drew strength from her love. He could make it because he was not alone. According to Mom, some days it required fifty hugs and kisses to get through his little books.

But as time went on he began to like the idea of home schooling. He had his mom as a teacher, which meant special field trips and unhurried visits to the library. Why, he could even take his schoolwork to Gramzy's when the others had to report to school.

By October he was glad to be home-schooled. The added affection and encouragement had helped to build his self-esteem and made the challenge seem more possible to overcome.

When he was given an IQ Test he scored in the same range I did as a child, and his response was, "I'm normal. I'm like Gramzy, and she wrote books, so I'll be fine. Some day I'll be reading and writing books!" he concluded with not a small amount of relief.

One evening when Grandpa was taking care of the children and it was time for a bedtime story, he reached up into the bookcase and took one of Uncle Arthur's *Bible Stories* from the shelf. The book opened to a story about Jesus in His childhood. Grandpa found himself reading a sentence that caught Eric's attention as little else had! "Jesus' mother was His teacher," The Bible story read.

Immediately my husband caught the significance this particular story had to Eric's situation.

"Eric," he said. "Isn't it wonderful? Jesus' mother was His teacher too!" How sweet to see the light dawn in his eyes as he grasped how Jesus' learning experience paralleled his own.

Later, when his mother returned home, Eric was still awake. Hurriedly, he threw back the covers and ran down the steps. "Mom, Jesus went to home school too! Jesus' mother was His teacher too! Did you know that, Mommy?" Yes, she knew it, and she was very pleased to see how this knowledge made her son more comfortable with his own situation.

For Eric this was good news! For how could anyone go wrong if they were following in the path of Jesus? " 'My sheep listen to my voice; I know them, and they follow me. I give them eternal life, and they shall never perish; no one can snatch them out of my hand' " (John 10:27, 28, NIV).

24
GETTING IN THE GROOVE

*Remember, when life gets out of sync
remain calm; it's only a matter of time
before you'll be back in the groove.*

It was hard to believe that Ryan would soon be celebrating another birthday. It seemed like only a short time since I'd gone to spend a few days with him and his mom when he was just a week old. That first morning my daughter let me give her first-born his bath. When I was through I wrapped him in one of his soft new terrycloth towels and headed for the squeaky rocker in his bedroom.

This was the moment I had dreamed of! I was a grandmother and relishing every bit of it.

I attempted to put Ryan's head on my shoulder so that I could rock him for the very first time. But he refused to bend in that direction. Instead, arching his small back and pushing his head against my hand, he looked me straight in the eye with an intense gaze. Now, I knew that baby's eyes couldn't focus when they're seven days old, but his were looking directly into mine, and he appeared to be checking Grandma out!

And now as I sat in the stands, this first-born grandson was standing on a pitcher's mound pitching in a playoff game. I almost had to shake my head to be sure I wasn't dreaming. Ryan was almost thirteen, looking every bit like a fifteen-year-old, who was very serious about pitching a good game.

After pitching to a couple of batters and walking them, Ryan surprised all of us when he called out to his mother from the pitcher's mound, "Mom, I've lost my groove!" Now we all know that a pitcher is doomed to defeat if he or she loses their groove. So this was serious. We tried to keep straight faces, although we were smiling on the inside. Yes, Ryan looked the part of a full-grown ballplayer dressed in his uniform and playing under the lights. But when he recognized that he had lost his groove he still turned to his mom. Several other parents smiled at this exchange between a young pitcher, throwing balls instead of strikes, and his trust in his mom. Michael, his coach and stepfather, went out to the mound to reassure the pitcher.

How many times have we seen football players mouth the words "Hi, Mom!" after making a good play and knowing that the TV cameras were turned on them? Yes, no matter how old we get, it's natural to turn to Mom when we're struggling. Why? Because time has taught the blessed among us that Mom can be counted on when the going gets rough.

But there's Someone who is even more reliable than Mom is! Isaiah 49:15, says it this way: " 'Can a mother forget the baby at her breast and have no compassion on the child she has borne? Though she may forget, I will not forget you! See, I have engraved you on the palms of my hands' " (NIV).

25
FORCED OUT!

Everyone gets to participate in the new earth.

On one particular day I was filling in for Mom. And after calling for each of my daughter's three children from their schools, I found a comfortable seat in the shade of the front porch and watched them move into their after-school activities.

Soon a seven-year-old boy began to rally the neighborhood kids for a game of soccer in the street in front of his house. Quickly Heather slid off the steps from beside me and joined him, calling out to her brothers to come too. I watched with interest at the negotiations that took place as the youthful organizer tried to convince everyone he could to join in a game of soccer.

He was a patient lad, and in time, with the help of my granddaughter, he had enough kids to begin the game. He stood in the center, posturing himself as the captain. After all, wasn't this his idea, and didn't he have the soccer ball pinned to the blacktop with his right foot?

Just as the two sides began to line up, the self-appointed captain called out loud enough for everyone to hear, "No girls allowed!"

All of a sudden, the one who had helped him

74

rally the troops was sidelined. After his stinging words set in, Heather threw back her shoulders, and while fighting back tears, one of the star players hurriedly made her exit. Her feet punctuated each step as she passed me, heading straight up the stairs to her bedroom.

I was close on her heels. I did my best to console her. Each sob in her pillow tore at my heartstrings. I knew the stinging reality of rejection as a child and even as an adult. While I suggested that we do a variety of things together, it wasn't what she wanted. What she wanted was to be included—to be able to play the game!

I had just decided to give her a few minutes to work through her disappointment when I heard her mother's voice through the open window. Eric, Heather's younger brother, had spoken up to expose the dastardly situation, knowing full well that his mother would speak out for the disenfranchised. And she did.

"All of my children know how to play soccer," my daughter said. "And either the game is open to all who want to play or none of the Bowen kids will be playing." Well, Heather chose not to play in that particular game, but I have been at their house since then when the call to play soccer was not gender exclusive.

The gospel is clear. "There is neither Jew nor Greek, slave nor free, male nor female, for you are all one in Christ Jesus" (Galatians 3:28, NIV). Yes, inclusion is a beautiful word!

26

LOOKING OUT FOR GRAMZY

LESSON TWENTY-SIX:
Beware of evil in places you least expect it.

It was early summer, and Eric and I were on a crusade to get rid of the wasp's nests that seemed especially prevalent that year. One of their favorite places to build a nest was under the eaves of the house. We made a trip to the local farmer's co-op to buy a can of spray that shot deadly foam at quite a distance. Of course, this was great fun for an eight-year-old boy! It was like declaring war, going after the wasps with a vengeance. When I had reached as many as I could with the spray, we discovered that other nests, even mud daubers, still clung to the eaves of the house—especially at the highest points of the roof.

I told Eric that we'd have to wait for Grandpa to come home to rid ourselves of the last of the pests, but this was not to be. He came up with a variety of ways that we could finish the job before sunset and rest in peace. It mattered little that the solution that seemed most doable required me to make a spectacle of myself.

His solution involved an eight-foot stepladder and a tool made up of a broom with a mop handle taped securely to the end of it. When I climbed the ladder with Eric's 60-pound body as my support, I had a weapon ten feet long. The wasps should have fled at the very sight of this aerial act—but wasps are tough, and they hang in there until one of you loses.

Standing on the next-to-the-top step of the ladder, I balanced myself and then, with the mop end of my weapon, I undertook a minesweeping motion under the eaves. Surprise of surprises, we were quite successful! One success after another spurred us on to greater heights until I was on the top step reaching as far as I dared.

When I came off the ladder I didn't look to see how many of the neighbors were watching this war from behind their mini-blinds, but I was a hero in one little boy's eyes. Throughout the evening he relived the adventure with a great deal of enthusiasm. The two of us had made our home safe and wasp free!

I went into the house to recover and prepare something for the two of us to eat. And when I was just ready to call Eric for dinner, the kitchen door burst open, and there he stood in full stature bearing an urgent message for his grandmother.

"Gramzy, I just saved you from a lot of trouble!" he said. "Come here and I'll show you!" He motioned me to follow him. Just outside the kitchen door hangs an iron dinner bell that we ring to call the family to meals. Pointing inside the bell, Eric revealed danger lurking. A wasp was hovering over its hive. "Get back, Gramzy!" Eric said. "I think it's a mother wasp, and she's going to get mad at you!" But having conquered numerous similar nests earlier in the day I headed for a weapon. This time I took the handle of the broom and drove it up into the bell, crushing the wasp and bringing the hive down to the floor of the deck in one fell swoop. Eric came closer to examine the results of my efforts. "Look, Gramzy! The hive is full of baby wasps just ready to be hatched! Gramzy," he said with his eyes as big as saucers. "I saved you a lot of pain by looking in that bell. The next time you would have reached to ring the dinner bell these wasps could have stung you. Gramzy, you have to look for evil things that can hurt you in places you don't expect them!" He punctuated his sentence with a look of confidence.

Yes, Eric, evil does lie in wait in places we least expect it. That's the way Satan catches us off guard. And his sting is worse than that of a hornet with far more serious consequences. Eric was right. He had saved me a lot of grief, and I loved him for it.

27

ANOTHER WAY TO SAY "I LOVE YOU"

Remember how powerful a smile can be.

At first his hand was an infant's clutched fist, and then a tiny hand wrapped around Mommy's finger. However, it didn't take long before his little hands became affectionate, stroking Daddy's face or petting his puppy.

A beautiful fall afternoon found me doing something I had dreamed of for years—sitting on our backyard swing-for-two with my newest grandchild on my lap. After all, our son was forty years old when he became a father, so this little boy was a blessed addition to the three grandchildren we already had.

I turned Clay around on my lap so that I could have a one-way "conversation" with him. I chatted away playfully, enjoying his ever-changing facial expressions and an occasional broad smile or chuckle. I told him that one day he wouldn't be content to sit on my lap, but rather he'd want to be running around chasing his doggie. I also informed him that when he stumbles and falls Grandma Rose has "magic creams" that make boo-boos stop hurting in no time. Then he reached out with both hands and grabbed my cheeks and pulled me closer as if to have

79

a better look at the Grandma of "magic creams." Then one hand reached for my nose, something he could get a hold of, while his other tried determinedly to grasp a small brown spot on my cheek. But essentially it was his eyes that "talked," his larger-than-life blue eyes that would simply melt in an affectionate gaze. I chuckle to myself when I think how many little girls will blush over a smile from those blue eyes someday!

Obviously, at seven months of age Clay is not talking yet. However, his ability to convey affection without a vocabulary reminded me of the numerous times I'd communicated without words. In the late 1980s my husband and I spent a significant amount of time in the former Soviet Union. And because I couldn't speak Russian, I often relied on eye contact and sign language to get my message across.

Not a few times, while seated on the platform during a church service, I'd make eye contact with one of my Russian or Ukrainian sisters in the congregation. Our eyes would meet and often I'd be the first to smile. Americans have been free to smile at persons they don't know without raising suspicions. But citizens in Communist-ruled countries haven't had this luxury of free expression. So, what followed was often a moving experience. Cautiously, the recipient of my smile would smile back. To me it seemed as if a clay mask would begin to crack, allowing her smile to break free, releasing a flood of emotions ranging from bashful smiles to copious tears.

The language of love is communicated in many

ways—through touch, smiles, letters, phone calls, and gifts. And these expressions and gestures are the sweet honey of life.

I lingered on the swing until Clay fell asleep in my arms, savoring this sweet exchange of love and counting on many more in the future. I want to get to know what makes this little boy tick! I want to add my love to that of others who love him in hopes of softening some of the blows this world will serve up.

Can you imagine seeing Jesus face to face? I try to picture what it will be like, and daily I'm making plans to experience what my mind has only been able to imagine. No words will be necessary. Picture His loving eyes! I'm confidant they'll speak volumes when we have the opportunity to look into them. The Bible says so. "Your eyes will see the king in his beauty and view a land that stretches afar" (Isaiah 33:17, NIV).

Clay, Grandma wants you to experience looking into Jesus' eyes. Yes, more than anything else—this is what I desire for you, little one!

28
TOP-SECRET TIME!

LESSON TWENTY-EIGHT:

Children still desire time with their parents and grand-parents even if they can't admit it to their friends.

It's always very special when you can spend time with one or two of your grandchildren and actually be able to have meaningful conversations. Someone said that becoming a grandmother ranks right up there with becoming a mother, only more fun and less work! Having experienced both, I agree!

This was the case one particular evening. I was going to be home alone with Ryan and Eric. At the dinner table Ryan asked what we were going to do after dinner. I said, "What would you like to do?"

"How about playing a table game, Grandma?" he responded.

"Sure, that sounds like a great idea!" I agreed. It didn't take us long to clear the table and load the dishwasher in readiness to play the game.

"Grandma, would you like to play Baseball Monopoly?"

"Sure," I said, relieved that it was a game I was familiar with. I noticed that the boys were carrying some folding lawn chairs from the garage to the lower level of the house, to Ryan's room. I asked, "Aren't we going to play here on the kitchen table?"

"No, Grandma. I want to play in my room." Ryan replied. Wow! Eric and I were getting invited into our teenager's inner sanctum for a game of Baseball Monopoly! When I came downstairs I discovered that Ryan had placed the three chairs around one of the corners at the bottom of his bed. And the game was neatly spread out ready to be enjoyed. I looked around. I was surrounded by some of the most notable Yankee baseball players of all time—in pictures, of course. And there was even a "bobbing head doll" of Orioles great Cal Ripkin over my right shoulder. Oh, and Derek Jeter was bobbing away on the nightstand. Wow, I thought. The bobbing heads have returned! They had been popular when our children were young.

"It's very nice of you to invite us to your room, Ryan." I began. "I haven't spent much time in your room, but it's very comfortable."

"Thank you, Grandma," he said as he continued to count out the Monopoly money. We rolled the dice and began play. The boys sympathized with me when I ended up in Jail two times in a row and celebrated with me when I got to "Pass GO" and collect $200.

We were busy buying up property and baseball teams as the game progressed, when the phone rang. It was Ryan's friend, Anthony. Ryan's mother had told me that he could spend the night with his friend if his mother agreed. Anthony would be calling after dinner, she said. The following day was teacher's conferences, so special privileges were on the table.

Ryan answered, and I could tell by his conversation that the sleepover had been approved. And then I heard him say, "Anthony, how late do you think your father could pick me up? Do you think he could come around eight-thirty?"

"Why so late?" Anthony inquired.

"Well, I have company, and we're in the middle of a game," Ryan answered.

After they agreed on the time Anthony would come for him, Ryan returned to the game without a word. I tried to keep my mind on the game in front of me, but my emotional heart melted into a puddle. My size-eleven-shoed, thirteen-year-old grandson still enjoyed spending time with his grandma enough to postpone going to his friend's. Wow!

I couldn't wait to tell his mother and grandfather. We all agreed that Ryan remains close to us because we've spent so much time with him since he was an infant. And we'll continue to be there whenever we can fit in, because first-borns are special, and teens need grandmas and grandpas too! Think about it: Families live on and pass on the family legacy through the stories we tell our children and grandchildren.

"From everlasting to everlasting the Lord's love is with those who fear him, and his righteousness with their children's children—with those who keep his covenant and remember to obey his precepts" (Psalm 103:17, 18, NIV).

29
MY GRANDMA, THE AUTHOR

LESSON TWENTY-NINE:
Your grandchildren know more about you than you think they do.

Heather's fifth-grade class was reading a book out loud—just as our First Lady, Laura Bush had recommended. After the class completed each chapter, the teacher would give the students questions to which they had to provide answers.

When the class finished the book they were reading the teacher passed out an additional assignment. Each of the students was to write to an author and ask the writer some questions. The responses would be shared with the class.

On the way to school one day, Heather said to her mother, "I have another assignment I need to do. I have to write to an author."

"Well, that sounds interesting, Heather," my daughter responded. "Have you given any thought to which author you'd like to write to?"

Without a moment's hesitation Heather said, "Yes, Mom. I'm going to write to Grandma Rose." My daughter came home after taking Heather to school and phoned to tell me that my only granddaughter was going to be writing to me—her choice of an author.

A couple of days later the teacher asked the class how many had decided which author they were going to contact. One of the first hands to be raised was Heather's. "I'm going to write to my grandma," Heather told the teacher.

"Well, is your grandmother an author?" the teacher inquired.

"Oh, sure, she's written books. In fact, she's writing one about me, and it will be published this spring. When it's done, I'll bring you one!" Not only was her grandma an author, but she was the subject of one of her books. How could you top that?

It pleased me when I realized that my granddaughter not only knew me as Grandma Rose, but she also knew something else that made me unique. And now she was drawing on my love for writing to fulfill a class assignment. How rich!

One day Ryan asked, "Grandma, why do you always write 'Jesus' kinds of books? Why don't you write a book about dinosaurs or something?"

I smiled and told him, "Well, I've spent my life working for Jesus. That's where my experience is. I've never had a keen interest in dinosaurs, Ryan. There are others who are much more qualified than I am to write about dinosaurs!"

Like Heather, I go to the Author when I face a challenging assignment. I call on my heavenly Father because I know Him personally and He has inspired sixty-six books. And they're all bestsellers.

Their action-oriented accounts include miracles, love stories, prison escapes, wars, stonings, healings, a life sketch of the greatest Man who ever lived on this earth, and prophetic guidance for the future!

I'll never forget placing children's Bibles in the Russian language in the hands of Russian, Ukrainian, Moldovan, Latvian, and Uzbek children and watching their responses. With nearly audible reverence they held a Bible, in their language, in their hands. And their little faces beamed with indescribable joy. It was overdue meat for the hungry, bread for little souls. And when I stood and looked into the faces of their parents I saw tears coursing down their cheeks. It was too good to be true. I want my grandchildren and yours to have this same thirst for God's Word. Because "all Scripture is God-breathed" (2 Timothy 3:16, NIV).

30

OUR EVER-PRESENT HEAVENLY FATHER

LESSON THIRTY:

When we call on the name of Jesus He will rebuke the devil and his angels.

My daughter's two boys have always had a fear of the dark. As long as I can remember they wanted an escort wherever they went in the dark.

One summer evening while visiting us, Eric, who was eight years old at the time, decided that he wanted something from his downstairs bedroom. Now it's true that his room is at the far corner of the lower level of our home—making it the longest distance between him and his mother, who was loading the dishwasher in the upstairs kitchen.

"Come with me, Mom," he pleaded. "You know how afraid I am in the dark! Please come with me!"

In her continued effort to help her youngest child conquer his fear of the dark, my daughter encouraged him to make the journey alone by telling him that she would converse with him all the while he was gone. Lifting his chin and looking into his eyes she told him that she would talk to him all the way down and back. If he listened he would be able to hear her voice and be assured that he was not alone. Just when she thought she had convinced him and began to talk to him in a reassuring tone of voice, she overheard him saying a phrase over and over as he hastily made the trip down the stairs to his bedroom.

Drying her hands, she made her way to the top of the stairs and strained to hear what Eric was chanting as he made the return trip at full speed. "I believe in Jesus! I believe in Jesus!" he said over and over again as he began to run up the stairs.

"Eric," Heidi said. "I told you that I would talk to you all the way there and back!"

"Yes, I know, Mom, but what good would that do? I needed to talk to Someone who really had the power to protect me if there were any bad guys downstairs."

Although we've never harbored any bad guys at our house, we praised God that Eric knew where to go for the real power!

God's Word makes a promise to Eric and all of His children in James 4:7, 8, (NIV). "Submit yourselves, then, to God. Resist the devil, and he will flee from you. Come near to God and he will come near to you." When we consider these words, Eric's decision to rebuke the devil by repeating "I believe in Jesus" was undoubtedly his best defense!

THE CHRISTMAS TRAIN IS COMING!

LESSON THIRTY-ONE:

Healthy family traditions can encourage strong family ties.

Children are doubly blessed when they have two sets of patri-arks and matri-arks that love them. Our grandchildren are so blessed. Ryan, Heather, and Eric also have Grandpa George and Grandma Kay, their Florida grandparents. And Clay has grandparents Sharon and Stu, and Chester and Lori, who love him dearly too.

Having had very supportive grandparents myself, I looked forward to the role. Although it required years of patient waiting to achieve, my role was rather simple. I just had to sit back and wait for the news: "You're going to be a grandma!" Now, in our son's case those were words I wasn't sure that I'd ever hear! But I did, and little Clay was sure worth the wait.

I had a German grandmother, my mother's mother, Grandma Jennie; and a Swedish one, my father's mother, Grandma Amelia. We grew up going to the same little church with both sets of my grandparents. One was a small, reserved woman, and the other was a grandma with a large lap who was the life of the party. As their granddaughter, I guess I'm a bit of both.

Since we all lived in the same small town of Manistee, Michigan, we used to alternate spending Christmas Eve at our grandparents' homes. At my father's parents' home, Grandma Amelia would entertain us with stories of parenting twelve children.

A Christmas tradition that I've carried on as a grandmother came from my maternal grandmother, Jennie. One year she delighted her seven grandchildren with a handmade Christmas train. Made from cardboard boxes covered with bright-colored foil, the train wound itself around the foot of the Christmas tree. We were all so delighted with it that she continued to make the Christmas train for a number of years.

Now, forty-five years later, my grandchildren enjoy a Christmas train when they come to our house. In fact, it's time to begin looking for the foil I want to cover the boxes with to make up this year's train. Once again it will have a few more cars because my sister Amy's family, including four young girls, will be celebrating the holidays with us, and they're "train converts" too.

Although the train takes time to make with an engine complete with a headlight and cowcatcher, it serves multiple purposes. It keeps the gift exchange organized and helps the children know where to go when it's their turn to open a gift. And it's pretty and fun!

For two years I made a red caboose and put the name "Baby Otis" on the side of the car for "seed." And it worked! This year Baby Otis is no longer anonymous. He's Clayton Brennan Otis, our newest grandchild.

In today's society, when families are scattered, healthy family traditions may be more important than ever before. Traditions are the glue that helps to bind the family together by providing pleasant memories that will linger forever.

While we know that Jesus was not born in December, we do know that He was born in a stable in Bethlehem to parents of Jewish heritage. He was born in the most humble of circumstances, so that it would be clear that He was the Redeemer of all persons regardless of class or ethnicity. Hallelujah! He is ours! We have a Redeemer who grew to manhood, preached love, healed the broken, and died on a cross so that our "broken-ness" could find healing. And instead of living for two or three generations we can enjoy eternal life in the new earth with the Babe from Bethlehem—who surely had grandparents who doted over him too.

"When Simeon saw the baby, he knew He was the Messiah. He gently took the baby from Mary's arms, held Him up and praised God saying, 'O Lord, you have kept your word to me. You have let me see the Instrument of your salvation which you are sending to us to save all peoples' " (Luke 2:28-31, The Clear Word).